JAPANESE ART

FUN AND EASY ART FROM AROUND THE WORLD

ALEX KUSKOWSKI

Super Sandcastle

An Imprint of Abdo Publishing
www.abdopublishing.com

Consulting Editor, Diane Craig,
M.A./Reading Specialist

VISIT US AT WWW.ABDOPUBLISHING.COM

Published by Abdo Publishing, a division of ABDO, PO Box 398166, Minneapolis, Minnesota 55439. Copyright © 2015 by Abdo Consulting Group, Inc. International copyrights reserved in all countries. No part of this book may be reproduced in any form without written permission from the publisher. Super SandCastle™ is a trademark and logo of Abdo Publishing.

Printed in the United States of America, North Mankato, Minnesota
062014
092014

THIS BOOK CONTAINS RECYCLED MATERIALS

Editor: Liz Salzmann
Content Developer: Nancy Tuminelly
Cover and Interior Design and Production: Mighty Media, Inc.
Photo Credits: Aaron DeYoe, Shutterstock

The following manufacturers/names appearing in this book are trademarks: Rit®, Anchor®, Mod Podge®, Sharpie®, Jerzees®

Library of Congress Cataloging-in-Publication Data
Kuskowski, Alex., author.
  Super simple Japanese art : fun and easy art from around the world / Alex Kuskowski ; consulting editor, Diane Craig, M.A., reading specialist.
     pages cm. -- (Super simple cultural art)
  Audience: Ages 5-10.
  ISBN 978-1-62403-281-3
1. Handicraft--Juvenile literature. 2. Japan--Civilization--Miscellanea--Juvenile literature.
I. Craig, Diane, editor. II. Title. III. Series: Super simple cultural art.
  TT160.K8743 2015
  745.50952--dc23
                         2013043462

Super SandCastle™ books are created by a team of professional educators, reading specialists, and content developers around five essential components—phonemic awareness, phonics, vocabulary, text comprehension, and fluency—to assist young readers as they develop reading skills and strategies and increase their general knowledge. All books are written, reviewed, and leveled for guided reading, early reading intervention, and Accelerated Reader® programs for use in shared, guided, and independent reading and writing activities to support a balanced approach to literacy instruction.

TO ADULT HELPERS

Children can have a lot of fun learning about different cultures through arts and crafts. Be sure to supervise them as they work on the projects in this book. Let the kids do as much as possible on their own. But be ready to step in and help if necessary. Also, kids may be using glue, paint, markers, and clay. Make sure they protect their clothes and work surfaces.

KEY SYMBOL

In this book you may see this **symbol.** Here is what it means.

SHARP!
You will be working with a sharp object. Get help.

TABLE OF CONTENTS

JAPANESE BONSAI

The bonsai is a tiny tree grown in a container.

COOL CULTURE

Get ready to go on a **cultural** art adventure! All around the world people make art. They use art to show different **traditions** and ideas. Learning about different cultures with art can be a lot of fun.

Japan is an island country. It has many traditions. Japanese paper folding is a popular art form. It is over 300 years old!

Learn more about Japan! Try some of the art projects in this book. Get creative with culture using art.

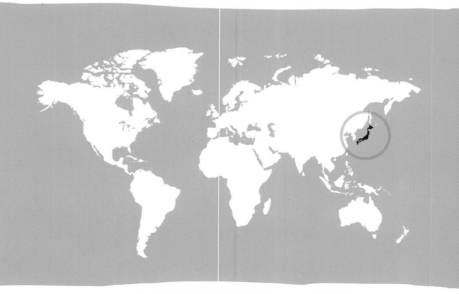

Before You Start

Remember to treat other people and **cultures** with respect. Respect their art, **jewelry**, and clothes too. These things can have special meaning to people.

There are a few rules for doing art projects:

▶ **PERMISSION**

Make sure to get **permission** to do a project. You might want to use things you find around the house. Ask first!

▶ **SAFETY**

Get help from an adult when using something hot or sharp. Never use a stove or oven by yourself.

ART IN JAPANESE CULTURE

People in Japan create many beautiful things. Some are for everyday use. Others are for special occasions. The **designs** in Japanese art often have special meanings.

 Block printing is used in Japan to make art, plays, and books.

 Temari balls are a kind of Japanese toy. Temari means "hand ball" in Japanese.

 Kokeshi are a kind of doll from northern Japan. Many are made of painted wood.

 Geta are **traditional** Japanese **sandals**. They are often worn with a **kimono**.

 Origami is the Japanese art of paper folding. People fold all kinds of shapes from paper.

 Bento boxes are packed meals that are sometimes arranged to look like art.

 Koi are a kind of Japanese fish. In Japan, people fly wind socks that look like koi for Children's Day.

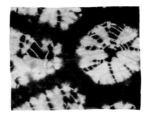 Shibori is an ancient Japanese way of dyeing cloth with patterns. It's been around since the eighth century!

WHAT YOU NEED

acrylic paint, paintbrush & foam brush

American cheese slices

black olives

bucket & rubber gloves

cardboard sheet, tube & oval box

carrots & lettuce

chenille stems

crackers

craft glue & tape

cupcake liners

dark blue Rit dye

drinking straws

googly eyes

hamburger buns

jingle bell & ribbon

key ring

large screws

laundry soap

lunch meat slices

measuring cups & spoons

Mod Podge

newspaper

patterned & origami paper

plastic lunch container

pushpin & wooden clothespin

ruler, ball-point pen & marker

sand & small rocks

scissors

small planter

stick

strawberries

string, yarn & yarn needle

Styrofoam ball & Styrofoam tray

thin metal wire

tissue paper & plain paper

vegetable peeler, sharp knife & cutting board

white cotton T-shirt

JAPANESE TIE-DYE

Make a shirt that looks like rippling water!

WHAT YOU NEED

white cotton T-shirt

soap

water

large screws

string

scissors

rubber gloves

dark blue Rit dye

bucket

DIRECTIONS

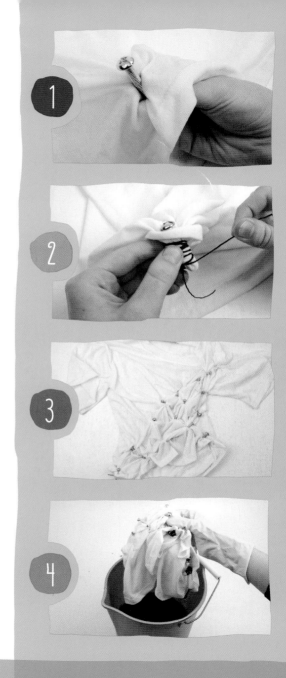

1. Wash the shirt in soap and water. Lay the shirt out flat. Put a screw on top of the shirt. Fold the shirt around the screw.

2. Wrap a piece of string around the **material** covering the screw. Tie the string in place. Cut off any extra string.

3. Wrap and tie more screws the same way. Tie each screw on a different part of the shirt.

4. Put on rubber gloves. Prepare the dye in the bucket. Follow the instructions on the dye box. Put the shirt in the bucket. Dye the shirt according to the instructions on the dye box.

5. When finished, rinse the shirt in running water. Stop when the water is clear. Let the shirt dry.

PAPER BOX ORIGAMI

Box it up with paper!

origami paper

DIRECTIONS

1   Place the paper pattern side up. Fold the paper in half to make a rectangle. Unfold the paper. Fold the paper in half the other direction. Unfold it. Turn the paper over.

2   Fold the four corners of the paper to the center.

3   Fold the left and right sides in so they meet in the center. Then fold the top and bottom sides in so they meet in the center. Unfold the paper until only the left and right corners are folded in.

4   Fold the left and right sides up. Push the tops of the folded-in corners together.

5   Fold the top corner over to hold the sides in place.

6   Turn the paper around. Repeat steps 4 and 5 with the remaining unfolded corner.

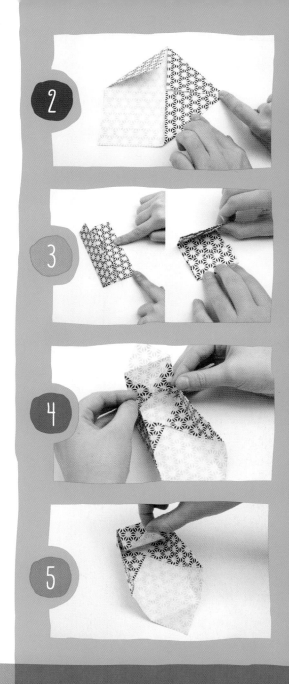

KEY CHAIN DOLL

Take this doll with you everywhere!

WHAT YOU NEED

wooden clothespin

acrylic paint

paintbrush

marker

Mod Podge

pushpin

thin metal wire

scissors

ruler

key ring

DIRECTIONS

1. Paint the face and hair on the top of the clothespin. Let the paint dry.

2. Use the marker to draw a **kimono** on the clothespin. Paint the kimono. Let the paint dry. Paint the clothespin with a coat of Mod Podge. Let it dry.

3. Have an adult help you make two holes on top of the clothespin with the pushpin.

4. Have an adult help you cut a piece of wire. Make it ½ inch (1.3 cm) long. Bend the wire. Push the ends into the holes on the clothespin. Put dots of glue over the holes. Let the glue dry. **Attach** the key ring through the wire **loop**.

QUICK TIP: Decorate the kimono! Paint on a fun **design**.

RINGING YARN BALL

Jazz up your room with a temari ball!

Styrofoam ball

craft glue

blue, yellow, and red yarn

scissors

yarn needle

ruler

jingle bell

ribbon

DIRECTIONS

① Put a little glue on the Styrofoam ball. Glue one end of the blue yarn to the ball.

② Wrap the yarn around the ball. Cover the ball with yarn.

③ Cut the yarn. Thread the yarn through the needle. Stick the needle under the wrapped yarn. Pull it all the way through. Remove the needle. Tie the yarn in a knot to hold it in place. Cut off the extra yarn.

4　Cut 12 feet (3.7 m) of yellow yarn. Thread the yarn through the needle. Stick the needle under a **strand** of blue yarn. Pull it all the way through. Remove the needle. Tie the yellow yarn around the blue yarn.

PROJECT CONTINUES ON THE NEXT PAGE

DIRECTIONS (continued)

(5) Wrap the yellow yarn around the ball in one direction. Use the needle to bring the end of the yellow yarn under the wrapped yarn. Remove the needle. Tie the yarn in a knot to hold it in place. Cut off the extra yarn.

(6) Cut 6 feet (1.8 m) of red yarn. Thread it through the needle. Stick the needle under a **strand** of yellow yarn. Pull it all the way through. Remove the needle. Tie the red yarn around the yellow yarn.

(7) Wrap red yarn over the yellow yarn. Tie the yarn in place. Cut off the extra yarn.

DIRECTIONS (CONTINUED)

8. Cut 6 inches (15 cm) of blue yarn. Put the bell on the yarn. Thread one end of the yarn through the needle.

9. Stick the needle under the blue yarn on the ball. Pull it all the way through. Remove the needle. Tie the yarn in a knot to hold the bell in place.

10. Cut a ribbon 12 inches (30.5 cm) long. Thread it through the needle. Stick the needle under the blue yarn on the side opposite of the bell. Pull it all the way through. Remove the needle. Tie the ends of the ribbon together.

KOI WINDSOCK KITE

Fly your fish kite with your friends!

WHAT YOU NEED

cardboard

scissors

ruler

cardboard tube

orange paint

foam brush

orange tissue paper

craft glue

googly eyes

string

tape

stick

DIRECTIONS

1   Cut two fish fin shapes out of cardboard. Make them each 2 inches (5 cm) long.

2   Paint the fins and the cardboard tube orange. Let the paint dry.

3   Cut eight strips of tissue paper 1 inch (2.5 cm) by 9 inches (23 cm). Glue the strips to the inside of one end of the tube. Let the glue dry.

4   Glue the googly eyes near the other end of the tube. Glue the cardboard fins on either side of the tube. Angle the fins **outward**. Let the glue dry.

5   Cut two pieces of string 12 inches (30.5 cm) long. Tape both ends of one string inside the tube on opposite sides. Tie one end of the second string to the middle of the first string. Tie the other end of the second string to the stick.

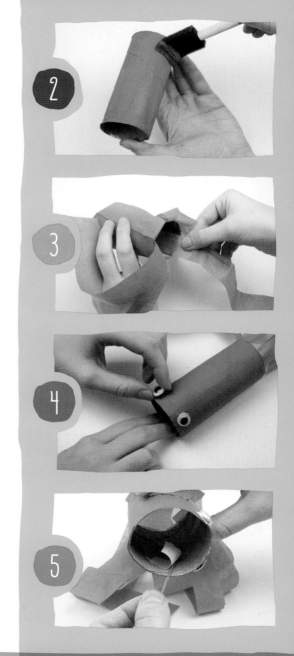

BUILD-A-BONSAI

Make a tabletop tree that lasts forever!

small planter

sand

10 brown chenille stems

scissors

green tissue paper

ruler

craft glue

small rocks

DIRECTIONS

1 Fill the planter with sand.

2 Twist six chenille stems together. Start twisting 2 inches (5 cm) from one end. Twist them together for 5 inches (12.7 cm). Then twist two of the stems together to make a branch. Make two more branches the same way.

3 Cut the other four chenille stems into pieces. Make the pieces different lengths. Twist the pieces onto the branches to make more branches.

4 Cut the tissue into 1-inch (2.5 cm) squares. **Crumple** the squares. Put a dot of glue on a branch. Press a tissue square to the glue. Glue tissue squares to all of the branches. Let the glue dry.

5 Bend the bottoms of the chenille stems. Bury them in the sand. Use rocks to help hold the tree in place.

JAPANESE SANDAL CASE

Store little things in this cute case!

WHAT YOU NEED

black chenille stems

scissors

oval cardboard box

patterned paper

Mod Podge

foam brush

DIRECTIONS

1. Twist two black chenille stems together. Cut the twisted chenille stems in half.

2. Have an adult help you make three small holes through the box top. Make a hole on each side. Make the third hole at one end.

3. Push one end of both stems through the hole at the end of the box top. Push the other end of each stem through a hole on the side.

4. Turn the box top over. Bend the ends of the stems to hold them in place.

5. Brush Mod Podge on the sides of the box. Cover with patterned paper. Smooth it out. Cut off any extra paper. Let the glue dry.

BEAUTIFUL BLOCK PRINT

Carve up some cool art!

thin Styrofoam tray

scissors

ball-point pen

newspaper

foam brush

paint

plain paper

DIRECTIONS

1 Cut off the sides of the tray.

2 Use the pen to draw on one side of the tray. Press hard enough to scratch the Styrofoam.

3 Cover your work area with newspaper. Lay the Styrofoam on the newspaper. Brush a thin layer of paint on the Styrofoam.

4 Carefully lay a piece of plain paper on top of the Styrofoam. Press lightly on the paper. Carefully lift the paper up.

LION BENTO BOX

Make a lunch you'll love to munch!

WHAT YOU NEED

carrots
vegetable peeler
sharp knife
cutting board
measuring cups & spoons
1 black olive
ruler
American cheese slices
drinking straw
hamburger bun
lunch meat slices
lettuce
plastic lunch container
cupcake liners
sliced strawberries
small crackers

DIRECTIONS

1. Peel a carrot. Cut off one round **slice**. Cut it into four pieces. Use the peeler to make ½ cup of carrot strips. Cut the olive in half **lengthwise**. Cut each half again lengthwise.

2. Cut two cheese circles 1 inch (2.5 cm) across. Cut two cheese triangles 1 inch (2.5 cm) across.

3. Cut a cheese circle 3 inches (7.6 cm) across. Cut off one-third of the circle. Use the straw to make holes in the cheese circle. Put three holes on each side.

PROJECT CONTINUES ON THE NEXT PAGE

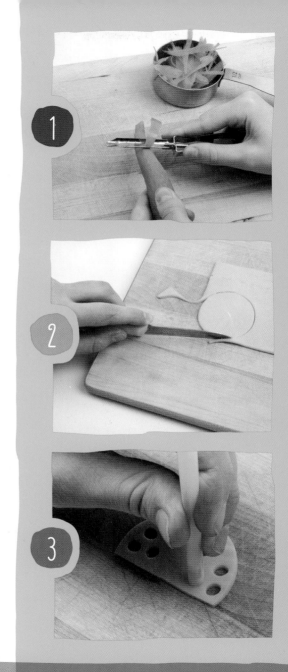

DIRECTIONS (continued)

(4) Open the hamburger bun. Put cheese, lettuce, and lunch meat on the bun. Put the top on the bun.

5 Put the **sandwich** in the lunch container. Put two cupcake liners next to the sandwich.

(6) Put the carrot strips around the sandwich.

(7) Add eyes. Put the small cheese circles on the sandwich. Put a piece of the olive on each cheese circle.

DIRECTIONS (CONTINUED)

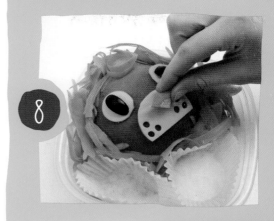

8. Add a nose. Put the cheese **slice** with the holes below the eyes. Put a piece of carrot near the top.

9. Add ears. Put the cheese triangles above the eyes.

10. Fill the cupcake liners with strawberries and crackers.

GLOSSARY

attach – to join or connect.

crumple – to crush or bend something out of shape.

culture – the ideas, art, and other products of a particular group of people.

design – a decorative pattern or arrangement.

jewelry – pretty things, such as rings and necklaces, that you wear for decoration.

kimono – a loose robe with wide sleeves worn in Japan.

lengthwise – in the direction of the longest side.

loop – a circle made by a rope, string, or wire.

material – woven fabric or cloth.

outward – away from the center.

permission – when a person in charge says it's okay to do something.

sandal – a kind of shoe that is held on with straps.

sandwich – two pieces of bread with a filling, such as meat, cheese, or peanut butter, between them.

slice – a thin piece cut from something.

strand – one of many threads or parts of a thread that make up something larger.

tradition – a belief or practice passed through a family or group of people.